AMAZING ANIMALS

ANACONDAS

BY ASHLEY GISH

CREATIVE EDUCATION • CREATIVE PAPERBACKS

Published by Creative Education
and Creative Paperbacks
P.O. Box 227, Mankato, Minnesota 56002
Creative Education and Creative Paperbacks
are imprints of The Creative Company
www.thecreativecompany.us

Design by The Design Lab
Production by Blue Design
Art direction by Graham Morgan

Images by Getty Images/Daniel Cardenas/Anadolu, 17, Julian Gunther, 5, Mark Newman, 2, MB Photography, 13, Nathaniel Williams, 9, Paul Starosta, 14, simonkr, 18; Shutterstock/ chrisbrignell, cover, 1; Unsplash/Bofu Shaw, 21; Wikimedia Commons/Alexander Gerst, 23, Aramburu Carlos, 6, Daniel Kraft, 20, Daniel10ortegaven, 16, Fernando Flores, 10, jorgehenao, 8, Patrick JEAN / muséum d'histoire naturelle de Nantes, 7

Library of Congress Cataloging-in-Publication Data
Names: Gish, Ashley, author.
Title: Anacondas / Ashley Gish.
Description: Mankato, Minnesota : Creative Education and Creative Paperbacks, [2026] | Series: Amazing animals | Includes bibliographical references and index. | Audience: Ages 6-9 | Audience: Grades 2-3 | Summary: "Dive into the world of anacondas with this this engaging zoology title for elementary-aged readers. Explore anacondas' habitats, diets, and unique behaviors, and uncover the myths and legends surrounding these incredible snakes"— Provided by publisher.
Identifiers: LCCN 2025011362 (print) | LCCN 2025011363 (ebook) | ISBN 9798895810514 (library binding) | ISBN 9798896800040 (paperback) | ISBN 9798895811771 (ebook)
Subjects: LCSH: Anacondas—Juvenile literature
Classification: LCC QL666.O63 G57 2026 (print) | LCC QL666.O63 (ebook)
LC record available at https://lccn.loc.gov/2025011362
LC ebook record available at https://lccn.loc.gov/2025011363

Printed in China

Table of Contents

Anacondas are big, tropical snakes that live around water. There are five kinds of anacondas. They are the northern green, southern green, yellow, dark-spotted, and Bolivian. Green anacondas are the biggest and most common.

Anacondas are slow on land but fast in the water.

Other predators do not bother adult green anacondas because of their size. Females are around 15 feet (4.6 meters) long. Males are smaller. They can grow up to 9 feet (2.7 m) long. Green anacondas weigh from 70 to 150 pounds (31.7 to 68 kilograms).

predator an animal that eats other animals

Anacondas hunt underwater along shorelines. They quickly attack animals that come to take a drink.

Anacondas **evolved** for life in the water. They can keep their eyes and nostrils just above the water, so they can breathe and see while hiding the rest of their body.

evolve change slowly over time

Anacondas are constrictors. This means they squeeze their **prey** *until it stops breathing.*

Anacondas eat animals like turtles, birds, capybaras, and caimans. Anacondas wrap their body around their prey to stop its breathing. Then they swallow their meal whole.

prey animals that are eaten by other animals

Anacondas live in South American rainforests and grasslands. They live near slow-moving rivers and streams. They sun themselves on branches hanging over the water.

Anacondas can live for around 10 years in the wild.

Green anacondas find mates between December and May. Many males may stay with one female for up to four weeks. Outside the mating season, anacondas do not see each other very much. They are solitary animals.

A group of anacondas is called a bed or a knot.

Anaconda mothers do not lay eggs. Babies, called snakelets, grow inside their mother. This way, they are protected from harm. After six months, anaconda mothers give birth to around 20 to 40 snakelets.

Anaconda snakelets are each about 2 feet (61 centimeters) long. They take care of themselves shortly after birth.

Anacondas have amazing abilities. They can hold their breath underwater for about 10 minutes. Their top speed underwater is 10 miles (16 kilometers) per hour. After a meal, an adult anaconda can go months without eating again.

Anacondas can take down larger animals, like deer or wild pigs.

Moving pets into the wild harms the pets and the wildlife in the area.

Many places sell anacondas as pets. Some anaconda owners in Florida released their pets into the wild. Now, there are anacondas in the Everglades, where they do not belong.

Everglades a wetland area in southern Florida

An Anaconda Tale

The Desana

people tell of an anaconda, called the Big Snake, who took the shape of a canoe. The snake-canoe traveled along the Amazon River. It created villages of people along the banks. This is how the people of Brazil came into being.

Read More

Bow, James. *Anacondas*. Mendota Heights, MN: North Star Editions, 2023.

Fenmore, Taylor. *Anacondas: Nature's Biggest Snake*. Minneapolis: Lerner Publications, 2024.

Terp, Gail. *Anacondas*. Mankato, MN: Black Rabbit Books, 2021.

Websites

15 Interesting Facts You Never Knew About Anacondas
https://www.beano.com/facts/animals/anaconda-facts
Learn some amazing facts about anacondas on Beano.

Anaconda
https://kids.nationalgeographic.com/animals/reptiles/facts/anaconda
Read more about anacondas on National Geographic Kids.

Anaconda
https://sdzwildlifeexplorers.org/animals/anaconda
Learn more about these "super squeezers" on the San Diego Zoo's website.

Index